DISCARD

D1275750

COINS AND MONEY
DIMES!

ROBERT M. HAMILTON

PowerKiDS
press™

New York

Published in 2016 by The Rosen Publishing Group, Inc.
29 East 21st Street, New York, NY 10010

Copyright © 2016 by The Rosen Publishing Group, Inc.

All rights reserved. No part of this book may be reproduced in any form without permission in writing from the publisher, except by a reviewer.

First Edition

Editor: Katie Kawa
Book Design: Katelyn Heinle

Photo Credits: Cover, p. 1 Lizzie Roberts/Ikon Images/Getty Images; cover, pp. 1, 5, 6, 9, 10, 13, 14, 17, 18, 21, 22, 24 (coins) Courtesy of U.S. Mint; cover, pp. 6, 9, 10, 13, 14, 17, 18, 21, 24 (background design element) Paisit Teeraphatsakool/Shutterstock.com; p. 5 (girl) wong sze yuen/Shutterstock.com; pp. 5, 6, 9, 10, 13, 22 (vector bubbles) Dragan85/Shutterstock.com; pp. 10, 24 (dollar bill) Fablok/Shutterstock.com; p. 14 (Roosevelt) UniversalImagesGroup/Universal Images Group/Getty Images; p. 17 (vector bubble) gst/Shutterstock.com; pp. 18, 21 (vector bubble) LAN02/Shutterstock.com; p. 22 (ball) © iStockphoto.com/bbostjan; p. 22 (price tag) Picsfive/Shutterstock.com.

Library of Congress Cataloging-in-Publication Data

Hamilton, Robert M., 1987-
 Dimes! / Robert M. Hamilton.
     pages cm. — (Coins and money)
 Includes bibliographical references and index.
 ISBN 978-1-4994-0751-8 (pbk.)
 ISBN 978-1-4994-0749-5 (6 pack)
 ISBN 978-1-4994-0498-2 (library binding)
 1. Money—Juvenile literature. 2. Coins—Juvenile literature. I. Title.
 HG221.5.H26 2015
 332.4'043—dc23
                              2014048193

Manufactured in the United States of America

CPSIA Compliance Information: Batch #WS15PK: For Further Information contact Rosen Publishing, New York, New York at 1-800-237-9932

CONTENTS

Dimes are coins.
We use coins to buy things.

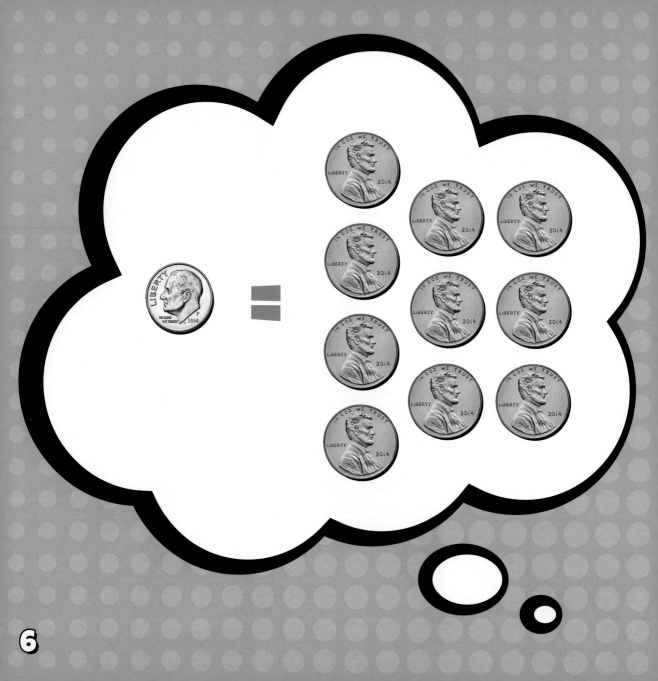

6

One dime is 10 cents. One dime is the same as 10 pennies.

If you have two dimes, how many cents do you have? Two dimes are 20 cents.

9

10

There are 10 dimes
in one **dollar**!

The dime is the smallest coin in the United States. All coins are made of metal.

DIME **PENNY** **NICKEL**

QUARTER **HALF-DOLLAR**

The dime has a man's face on the front of it. This is President Franklin D. Roosevelt.

The dime has an **olive branch** on the back of it. The olive branch stands for peace.

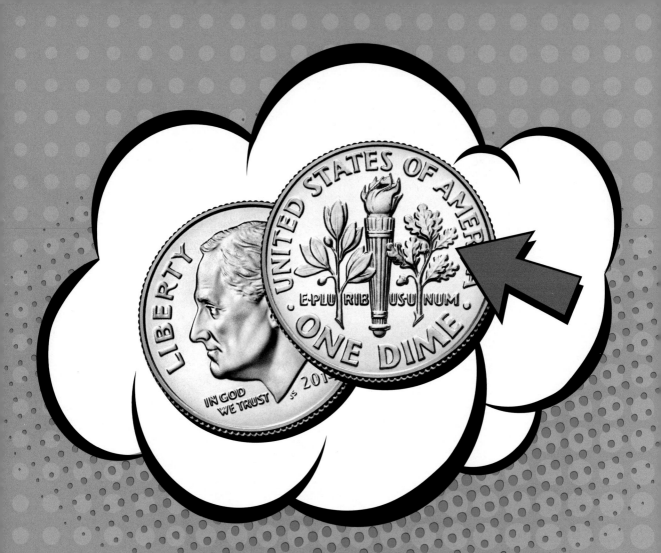

The dime has an **oak branch** on the back of it. The oak branch stands for strength.

The dime has a **torch** on the back of it, too. The torch stands for freedom.

This ball is 50 cents.
How many dimes is that?

CUYAHOGA CO. LIBRARY
123 EAST STREET
CLEVELAND OHIO **23**

WORDS TO KNOW

dollar

oak branch

olive branch

torch

INDEX

WEBSITES

Due to the changing nature of Internet links, PowerKids Press has developed an online list of websites related to the subject of this book. This site is updated regularly. Please use this link to access the list: www.powerkidslinks.com/cam/dime